Earth as our Ground
Sky as our Mirror

Earth as our Ground

Sky as our Mirror

Anne Linden Steele

Outset Press • New Mexico

2015

ISBN-10: 0692497595
ISBN-13: 978-0692497593

Outset Press

Santa Fe, New Mexico

Contents

Fruit   p. 15

What are we given?   p. 23

What is the Force that Grows Life   p. 25

An Ancient Forest   p. 31

Earth   p. 37

The Teaching   p. 45

Opposition   p. 51

Taking Root   p. 55

I don't know   p. 61

Mountains beyond Mountains   p. 67

Points of View Exercise   p. 71

Serendipity / Coincidence   p. 75

Tone   p. 81

Sky   p. 85

Injury   p. 89

Fate   p. 93

Soul   p. 95

What Stays   p. 99

Fate and Soul   p. 105

Fate and Soul Exercise   p. 107

To this day   p. 111

Heart   p. 117

A Man   p. 127

Kindness and Honesty   p. 133

Obstacle Exercise   p. 135

Giving   p. 139

What is our Contribution   p.141

Acknowledgements

I am immeasurably grateful to my parents Joan and Edward Steele who raised me in Fredonia, NY. I was lucky to grow with my cherished three brothers and a sister.

John Upledger's teachers and Hugh Milne taught me Craniosacral Therapy; Steve Schumacher, Jin Shin Do Acupressure; Mark Wolynn and especially Suzi Tucker taught me Family Constellation Work (FCW). This book's influence from Bert Hellinger, developer of FCW, is profound.

I am grateful to the clients who permitted their stories to be told in these pages and to the people of Louisville, KY who taught me throughout 20 years' private practice there. Thank you Mark, Paula and Beth for creating and deepening the path to Tulsa OK - and especially to Lynda Jacobs for your tireless organizing of my teaching of FCW there. Any skill in teaching gained was honed with your support.

I am forever grateful to Bruce for our children, to Steve for engaging in me my work in the world, and to this life for writing the questions and walking me toward their answers.

The forests of western New York, central Kentucky and now the high reaches of northern NM continue to teach.

Anne Linden Steele

April, 2015

annelindensteele.com

How do we begin life?

How does life begin us?

With enough to see us through

With little enough to want more

Fruit

What is it?

"It's an apple," my friend replied.

Are you sure?

"Yes - I don't like their taste but I am drawn to them, their shape, what's under the skin, how our juices meet the fruit and what happens to it then.

"I like the colors too - greens, reds, and yellows shimmer and swim inside its skin - just not the taste," he added.

There's more though - I see the haze of something behind it.

"Yes, it's a baby. She is writhing. Can you make it out?" he asked.

Not quite - it looks as if her image is held away, maybe pulled by time.

"It is - rather, she is."

What happened? Do you know her?

"Not any longer but I know her story. Shall I tell it to you?"

Yes. I said with interest.

"The child in the painting is my mother. Her birth was normal but her young life was not. Some torment held her and caused her legs to seize and her arms to flail. I was told she was inconsolable. Neither milk nor warmth nor motion helped.

"My mother met her grandfather the second day of her life. He was an osteopath. They see the body as a set of marvelous systems that are constantly interacting with the elements and with one another, all supported by some force much greater than medicine or even poetry.

"His name was Ben. My great-grandfather died when I was ten. A few times, I got to watch him when he worked.

"He would wait rather than talk, letting whatever was facing him approach. He told me he waited until he was shown either an image or a word and after that, a way to begin. Even at that point, he would remain still until he felt he was given permission to interact with the person or condition."

How would he know?

"He explained that in his journals. He wrote that he didn't know how he would know. His only task was to agree to be led, to follow, and to not seek an outcome.

"When my mother was born, my grandmother asked Ben to come quickly - sooner than either of them had planned. She wanted his understanding before anything else.

"When he arrived, Ben stood by the nursery door and gazed in.

"He wrote that he did the hardest thing first. He waited. He let himself settle amid what felt like a great wash of time and generations awakening inside him, his arms, his legs, his belly.

It gradually ebbed and brought him to a freshened, open space. Here, as if of its own accord, the image of an apple appeared.

"He told his daughter to bring him an apple, a sour one. It was early summer and my grandmother knew where they grew. My mother's father ran to the tree for his newborn daughter.

"When the apple arrived, Ben had a knife in hand. He peeled the apple and began to scrape its fruit onto a dish in the slowest, most tender of ways. He was in some kind of union with the fruit, as if whatever it held was coming forward.

"When he had scraped enough, he washed his hands and piled a tiny bit onto his smallest finger and gently tilted the fruit into my mother's mouth. The baby's focus charged toward what was new inside her.

"Her mouth puckered and rolled, guided by some organizing collection of instinct. As she swallowed, Ben fed her more, just a bit more. This continued for about 10 long minutes and then something happened. My mother's left knee began to relax from her chest. Her arms slowed their thrashing. She still cried out but her tone was less arched. Her eyes began to come into view, but only for moments.

"My great grandfather stood up and gave the knife, the apple and the small china dish to my mother's mother and suggested she continue feeding her newborn daughter in this way about every 30 minutes. 'I will,' she said.

"My great grandfather left the room quietly. He told my mother's father that a section of the child's intestine was likely twisted and that the tasting, the swallowing, the digesting of the fruit would help it un-kink. 'Once the child sleeps deeply you will know her insides have relaxed and she'll soon be ready for her mother's milk,' he noted. " 'Her mother will know this too.' "

How did he know the apple would help?

"He wrote that he didn't. He knew only to follow what he was shown.

"My mother lived until I was 30. She was taken by an illness no one could diagnose yet was peaceful when she died. When I went through her things I found Ben's journals and my grandmother's written memory of that day.

"I began painting after my mother died. She reaches me."

What are we given when we are born on this earth?

What was in place before institutions, beliefs, rules and groups became filters of our experience of being alive?

Our blood, our parents and ancestors, their strengths, their limitations and the accumulation of their pasts.

Earth, its capacity to include us, feed and house us, grow us.

Our soul's interest in learning more, in gathering wisdom.

Our willingness to be moved by what is beyond us.

Life is filled and defined by what is measurable and what is un-measurable.

We are given earth, family, several questions and an openness. In their company we will endure difficulty, contradiction, rally success and move through blinding confusions in order to gain answers that will expand our capacity to live more of life.

What kept our ancestors going? What keeps us going, moves us into each day, is beyond our clocks and pre-dates our cultures; what sets into place our experiences of birth, connection and of death?

What is active in stranger, kin, animal, air and every seed that somehow knows to open?

What is the force that grows life?

It seems we are held inside a harmonic, a collection of frequencies that variously moves, crashes in or gentles us as does a loved one's touch when checking whether we sleep. The tones are always in us registering both place and action in time and the cosmos.

This expression of life is as specific to each person, animal, object as is a snowflake, a star's position, and our collection of experiences. We are here with the participation of all of life. And all of life has come into being - in part - because each of us is here. All of life has come into being - in total - because earth is that generative.

As we enter this life, ever-drawing us forth and always waiting for us is our source of life, our ground: earth. Through earth we are given land that bears our food, plants that bear our oxygen, a sun that generates warmth and light, a cosmos that brings us night and rest, lakes and rivers that give us water and oceans that provide moisture and the currents that move wind, weather and more. An immense alchemy makes its way through the intangible as well as through matter.

While the forces that grow us remain unnamed, we can recognize them behind our experiences of attraction, loyalty, new ideas, building, humor and self-scrutiny. Each movement in life has as its origin a quality of the immeasurable. Subtle realms are constantly contributing to the ways we live, work, care for our family, create art, song and play.

Examples of the immaterial or subtle interacting with the material abound: a child is born from what began as an attraction between two people, ideas become a product that is greater than the sum of its parts, a flower opens, birdsong restores hope, food grows a body larger, beauty fosters tenderness, tenderness restores a sense of belonging. Honesty and kindness give us a standard around which we develop character.

We have countless creation stories and scientific theories reflecting our attempts to reconcile all that we are given while alive on earth with the question, just how did we get here? We may never solve this riddle. We may however come closer to needing it less once we allow our perceptions to widen into the various ways the subtle and matter create and engender vitality.

When religion separated time into on-earth and in-heaven (what is 'now' from the hereafter) and when science divided space into what can be reproduced in experiments from what arises of its own accord, we were left with only a portion of reality from which to construct our growth and development.

Missing was the experience of time beyond our clocks and the stillness of space beyond our measuring devices. Perhaps it is here that the forces that grow us begin.

From within religion and science's limited views, one can imagine that heaven became the goal and our time on earth, its nebulous proving ground. One can also imagine that as scientific proof became the goal, our time on earth developed into an increasingly mechanical experience, dependent upon the physical resources but disconnected from earth's organizing, generative alchemy.

Without an inherent respect for the source that keeps our lives living in every possible way, we've become takers. What are we missing or forgetting when the complexity of our lives has as its backdrop the supposition that earth is ours to use (up)?

It is a short walk from here to finding ourselves in the unstable posture or belief that we are in charge of earth - our source. This is impossible. Our source was here before each of us (came to divide it).

Division is by its nature, destabilizing (divide and conquer) because it excludes the whole of reality, the whole of nature. We live in a time when we are witness to the effects of instability in nearly daily occurrences of spontaneous or planned violence. One might observe that we are missing a fundamental security or relationship deep in our beings.

By contrast, a spontaneous peace alights when we remember our place, when we remember we are but a part of the whole and not the director of its elements.

Our imagined human position as administrator of life on earth may be our deepest expression of un-sustainability. Maintaining this posture removes us from participating in the generative nature of earth because we are owning rather than growing.

It is our nature to grow. All of life's nature is to grow. When we are separate from this inherent and organizing impulse, our appetites and our aggressions engage, perhaps to fill a hollow that deepens each time we turn away from our given nature. We are nothing if not viable aspects of earth's diversity.

Learning to live as contributors to and collaborators with earth may provide access to sustainability's deeper levels of wisdom.

We are startlingly similar - earth and self - and likely resource to one another.

An Ancient Forest

We'd driven far to reach its portal. It was a day of beauty: crisp air, mossy green underfoot, and sounds of creatures everywhere; maidenhair ferns just opening, their delicate leaves quaking as we walked near, the absolute presence of trees centuries old with no expectation of being taken by any force but the wind.

I want to tell you what happened:

As I walked up the trail, my companion commented about the state of our earth and humanity. He knows the earth as Gaia. "She doesn't need us. She will continue on, long after we humans have destroyed ourselves."

Often I simply listened when he spoke on this topic. It was different today. I said, "I'm not so sure."

"About which part?" he replied.

"About Gaia being separate from us, about the earth continuing on beyond our duration, as if our absence would not affect her."

"Tell me more," he said.

"Since no one knows the source of beauty, of joy, of peace, of right action, of abundance and diversity, it's possible that those sources are within both nature and us. That we are nature and that nature is not only the plants and the animals but us too. That we are suffering under a deep schism or split that positions humans as different or removed from Nature.

"It's possible that beauty in nature is generated through honesty.

"It's possible that joy occurs when a seedling silently makes its way through difficult growing conditions.

"Who can know whether stars are born because a child has extended his hand to a stranger in anguish?

"Maybe right action brings to nature its self-correcting capacity.

"That radiance is the effect of not only sunlight washing upon water but also of kindness touching defeat.

"A flower opens because even one person gives away what is cherished and whole meadows bend because a nation legislated equality.

And more -

"When we share we experience a sense of having more. What generates that? Perhaps animals who have done so forever.

"And this: we have a quiet place that arises in the company of one who has chosen self-restraint because Gaia has been practicing inclusion for eons.

"We feel better when we do what is right rather than what is self-serving because it is an instinct that arises out of countless community efforts from the bird and insect communities.

"This is all to suggest we are an integral part of nature and she of us. When we remove ourselves from the equation perhaps we remove a co-organizing aspect of the cosmos.

"As we rape ourselves and one another, we rape her. As we cherish each other/our nature, we cherish her/our Nature. Even the language is the same. As we walk in this habitat our experience is of greater communion; that we are home. How else to explain this?

"And how to return the favor of so much food, shelter, room and creation than to walk with opened hearts, to breathe our roots - both ancestral and woody - to follow her example of not taking more than we need, of making room, of giving. The qualities of forbearance and honesty bring a sense of deep ease, the same ease as I experience walking here in this forest. How can they be separate but in our minds? What could become possible if we release the beliefs that have decided such separateness?"

"It is hard," he said. "There is safety in the separation. I don't have to stand inside such an unknowable equation."

"And perhaps once we begin, an entirely new body of understanding will come forth. Maybe the equation seems immense only because we stand outside it."

Earth

Earth is more than our experience. And earth is our experience, our reference for the cycles of the seasons, birth, death, change, day and night. We live in response to earth's temperature, wind direction, rain, soil quality, minerals, currents and abundance.

In a way that is similar to the effect and influence of our family's blood circulating through us, earth's dynamic rhythm supports and interacts with our every movement.

We take and we take more for our survival, food, shelter, travel and mystery. We turn to heaven to mediate the vagaries of bounty, hoping sacrifices of all manner will right the balance of our having taken so much.

That heaven doesn't respond with direct action, leaves us in uncertainty, standing next to a vast universe and inside the cumulative effects of our actions.

What is our stance and our contribution toward the forces that support our lives? Our focus on sustainability has as its backdrop this question, whose answer can bring us closer to mutual renewal.

As human, we are given both matter and non-matter. Emotions, sensory input, the capacity to kill and the capacity to bring the new into being, occur beyond and within the confines of our perception of time, space and matter. Our four dimensions (time, height, length, depth) give us room, measurement and the sciences.

The measured worlds of time and space give us definition, limits and manageability while the unmeasured/immeasurable give us creation and all that is within and beyond us.

Theoretical physics is gradually meeting what mystics have experienced for centuries and what those who work in the subtle realms have experienced directly. Theoretical physics, healing work, martial arts and spiritual experience tell us there are more dimensions than the four mentioned above.

String theory posits there are at least 10 dimensions if the math behind it were calculated to the theory's logical conclusion. We have yet to name the other six, but life of its own accord daily brings experiences to us in the form of what is immeasurable yet palpable. The kindness of strangers, meditation, a child's first smile, the ways we inhabit or leave our bodies, emotions, beauty, honesty and fate, each has its reach into us and leaves a noticeable but unquantifiable effect.

When a helping practitioner is neutral and open to what is not yet known, a collection of forces arise out of the non-physical realms in the room.

A collaboration between client, practitioner and the unknown activates a potential for reconciliation of opposing forces within the client's body, mind or non-physical field, and leaves in its wake anexperience of equanimity. Access to multiple dimensions is gained and understanding more easily leads to wisdom. A sense of greater ease within a more coordinated matter/body occurs.

Often the "how" of this kind of experience is brushed off as unexplainable; yet the experience registers and stays with us. Martial artists know well the mysterious capacity gained when present time, absolute focus and release of agenda meet. A force that collects past present and future is unleashed as if a corridor were opened in the air.

It is possible that there are elements in matter we have not yet discovered, held there by and inside the other dimensions that are the change agents for life, discovery, and transformation. It is possible that the subtle and matter are equal partners, that the subtle and matter are one, and it is only our mind that holds them separate.

What makes matter utterly transformable? Chemistry would teach us that the right components brought together under the right conditions. And still - what is transformation's ignition? Alchemy would teach us that engaging the unknown, the not yet formed, the immeasurable, contributes to transformation's ignition. Earth's bounty, continually generated by a system that is beyond our human construct, would highlight kindness. How is it that we never forget our acts of cruelty if not that kindness inherently matters to the deeper reaches of life?

If kindness is part of earth's starter kit then perhaps honesty is part of ours. Honesty is an ever-present watchdog, always pulling on us when we've left its path. Because it is so ever-present, it must be known at least in frequency to the larger landscape we inhabit.

People, plants, animals and insects are responsive and receptive to what is beyond our known dimensions. We share earth, both what is knowable and what is as yet unknowable.

We can note that our pets at times seem to be conduits or messengers of a different realm, staring at a place in the room, barking or gesturing toward some non-physical presence. When we abuse our pets, it is as if some light goes out in our home and in ourselves. When we appreciate their presence, we feel buoyed by something beyond us.

"Plants are able to help us heal because they have lived through similar circumstances and are resonant with the cause, its toll and resolution," herbalist Matthew Wood teaches. In herbal medicine, a plant gathered with respect for its capacity will be more potent in its ability to transmit the requisite forces than one harvested by machine. Plants, like us it seems, are generous in the company of respect. Honesty communicates respect. We experience responsiveness as we care for plants.

In Wood's teaching, I find an explanation for Dr Edward Bach's observation that we always feel better after walking outside, and particularly in forests. His studies revealed each tree, each flower, each grass exudes a frequency that we experience as accompaniment in our difficulties. The Bach Flower Remedies continue to bring the forest's support of growth to many.

These experiences stand up to age-old assumptions that matter (such as clay and death) is inert and thereby separate from non-matter. Yet, in eating, loving, killing, bearing children and cultivating kindness, honesty, forbearance, meeting our difficulties to name a few, matter transforms.

Matter in fact, transfers itself; it does not lose itself, it does not evaporate. When we become conscious and respectful of this transfer, our appetites stabilize in new ways. Our impact within eco-systems lessens. We belong.

If we see matter and non-matter as separate we immediately lose both subtle and physical connections to our source earth and stand on the outside looking in. Once our minds reduce earth to inert matter, our source becomes a commodity and in a very direct way, we begin to devour our livelihood.

Conversely, if we see matter and non-matter as one and in constant and steady transformation, then we are able to hold earth as source of our livelihood. It is akin to seeing our parents as unrelated to our lives versus seeing our parents as the sources of our lives. It behooves us to learn the rhythms, response points and strengths and challenges of our origins.

Seen as transformation, death then becomes but an aspect of a larger growth. We are told we breathe the same air the dinosaurs did, revealing the immensity of earth's transformative use of all.

The Teaching

She appeared at my office tentative, ragged and utterly adrift. We met twice a week for hours. Her son had hung himself.

They had been close, shared a constancy of joy. And.

"How could I not have heard his need?

"I can only blame myself.

"I can't live right now."

The silences between each word were vast. A shadow clung both above and inside her face, her gait, her experience of absolute mistake.

No one would come close to her, the nightmare adrift in her eyes.

"Tell me the truth," she said.

The time together was as if in a dingy and only barely this side of deep waves. Her purpose was to tear away all pretense and denial her life had collected before his phone call, to somehow find who she was as mother and human being.

She would only take what was real. For a time self-blame served as rudder and anchor, both.

I learned to refrain from asking, How are you?

This day, her lungs are like magnets to my gaze.

Could you not blame yourself - just for a moment - to see what else is there?

It was a question that startled each of us.

She pushed it away even as her lungs redoubled their draw.

Just for a moment?

" . . . And lose everything?"

Yes

She did.

And in that moment a curtain fell

the air thinned

what it held, gave and opened in her

became a dimension that would

both dare her to stay and help her to stay.

We each felt it.

Her next words, barely whispered, taught me.

"This is how it felt when he was alive."

I believe you.

It was some time before this experience would become more trustworthy than self-blame and even more time before she chose to stay.

What she has gained her soul carries now.

It shows in her eyes, the additional moments she can bear the sight of mothers enjoying their children, a steadiness that can wait.

It shows in her gait - most steps - and in the deliberate way she uses her words, saying only what is true for her.

In her presence rests an arc that seems to reach back through her every experience and forward into tenderness, both unbidden and endured.

Opposition

It is possible to live inside a receptivity to what is a constant interplay between what we know and what we don't know; between the physical and the nonphysical worlds, between experiences that seem to oppose each other in daily living.

Examples include: I want to do this at 1pm and I want to do something else at the same time. I want to live in the mountains and my home is in the city. I want to stay and I want to go. My boss expects this and my integrity requires that.

Either-or creates a conflict in the place that understands that life has in fact already made room for each of us and our specific individuality. If there is room for me, deep down our sense of fairness tells us that there must be room for you, and each of our respective points of view. Exclusion brings us no lasting peace. Its regrettable effect is that we find ourselves fighting wars that have no completion.

We find ourselves in oppositions of all shapes and geographies without a way to reconcile them. It is a human conundrum which neither religion nor politics has solved.

Exclusion however, comes with its own elasticity - it will (eventually) become its opposite, that is, we will unconsciously become that which we consciously exclude or suppress. We see this over time in global tensions, relationships, family biases and historically when the formerly-conquered takes a position of power.

Alternately, both internally and by earth's example, when opponents make room for the other and for what is as yet unknown, a new dynamic opens that nourishes all.

Taking Root

The sidewalk is brittle, the sun has just set. There is a glow at the horizon. I am walking after dinner; at times my right foot drags and it takes mental effort to bring it into coordination with its partner. It is a small but regular nuance of this body's aging process.

Soon I forget it and look further into the air. It quickly engages me - the hydrangeas are in bloom and their beauty feels like tenderness touching my cheeks, entering my air passages. I am smiling from the inside and wanting my breath to hold what it is given forever.

My next steps bring me farther and into a honeysuckle's tendril. I cannot get over a flower whose sweetness slakes all wanting when tasted and then swallowed. This is a night of nights as its air descends and then lingers inside the day's heat. A bird cries as I approach a home whose door is slowing opening.

A ripple causes me to stop short of it. Uncertainty pours from the door. The front hallway's light pierces the dusky grey, Something not moving easily is evident here, even to a simple passerby.

They are a couple. A man, a woman to his left. A cat at their ankles. The cat hugs her legs unwilling to go out into the chilling air. He stands stiffly, neither moving forward nor back. I am wary of him and would rather move past unseen. I am uneasy with what presses into his joints, his chest, his jaw. The woman steps across the threshold with but one step and glances back toward him, perhaps aware of his rigidness. "Are you coming?" she asks.

His body remains frozen held in time's grip or by something more deeply anchored within. "I can't," he finally says in a gasping voice. "I will break." She nods and places her hand on his left arm. The cat slips back into the hallway. Without words, she holds his arm with the tenderness of one who has lived through disaster.

I am spellbound, standing just before the view from their front door, both witness and intruder. I cannot take my eyes away from what had frightened me about his rigidity and now relieves and somehow holds my heart in compassion and interest. She seems a partner of many years and separate years too, the way she does not push him and how she then turns to face him directly, her back to the street.

I watch her wait long moments until his eyes can meet hers. And when they do, he collapses into her arms. His tears are silent and revealed only by his body's tremor.

I wonder if I'd seen too much. Theirs is a dignity that softens me. She does not ask anything of him. Their bodies know one another from some shared devastation, this broken tenderness.

He asks nothing of her. What she gives she gives because she has it stored inside her life experiences. What he receives he takes in because he has no other choice, caught at a specific brink of some unthinkable event shaking loose what once had given him movement. They stay long moments.

I too in the shadows. I study his legs as they meet his feet. His knees wanting to buckle and his feet like magnets inside his shoes bracing his girth. They are all that stay frozen now, the rest of his body rests in the arms of this other human being's heart.

I turn back toward what had brought me to their sidewalk, the sun's glow gone now, knowing I had not seen too much. I quietly step away.

A fragrance like compassion travels a short silent distance and leaves its fullness. It stays with me. And remains there still, nourishing a place between words and breath, its own layer of tenderness and simple respect taking root.

I don't know

At the center of our lives is the unknown, the untried, the untested. It fuels our interests while at the same time defying our capacity to manipulate, dominate or direct it.

It is called many things by different cultures, myths, religions and philosophies. Regardless of its name, its quality remains the same: that which is beyond our knowing. We can recognize it by its presence and effect and then, only a little.

The unknown is responsive. When we acknowledge "I don't know," the air around us fills in just a bit. We relax.

Later, when new ideas, new ways and insights arise as if out of nowhere, we feel a little less alone in the very center of our lives.

Alternately, when we are afraid to not know, to be the 'dumb one,' effectively shutting out what we might learn, the air around us drains and we become anxious, feeling lost. Fear becomes its own multiplier until we distract ourselves with an appetite or acknowledge, "I need help. I don't know."

When we know too much, when life's riddle seems solved and our brilliance has seemingly cracked 'the code,' we begin to feel inflated, unsteady; we reach for some force of ego (that is, this brilliance came from me) to steady the ground and our view. Force of ego eventually knocks us over and we tumble back into our places of relative isolation.

Conversely, if we are able to acknowledge, "I don't know how this came to me," the conduit for the new remains open and generative. As are we.

Isolation would hold us in its arms forever were it not for this force finding us. Only the new/unknown can break isolation's lock. The remarkable thing is that it does, insistently, privately and quietly so. Especially when we are least teachable and most filled with unhappiness.

We experience an aspect of life pulling us back into some form of connection whether it's through ideas, insights, the kindness of a stranger, the car making it home safely when we are utterly consumed in thought, or an accident averted.

The new arrives through difficulty too. It changes our posture and point of view, giving us different variables to sort, juggle and integrate.

In both difficulty and relief, we are noticed and found. And the force that is 'finding us' provides a presence that replaces instability.

Within this experience of presence, the new is free to move. As are we.

'I don't know' is the place beyond our sight from whence ideas come.

It brings us what we are ready to learn, it offers insight, connects disparate experiences, and can spontaneously open the heart.

It is the origin of experiences that evoke the conclusion "I can't explain it."

It may influence dreams.

It is beyond clock time and beyond measured space.

It links us to the creative and the new.

It links the measured to the immeasurable.

It opens a passage to what is trying to emerge from inside duality/opposition.

Both matter and non-matter reach us here. Being alive has as its nature learning more.

It is the beginning of growth and comes in many forms.

I don't know acknowledges that the solution lies beyond me.

It is a way to respond to the complexity of input and provides a stance in deference to what is larger than we are.

It resets our mind and often our heart.

It is our place in relation to earth.

It is a bridge that opens the lock of duality, that acknowledges something is missing.

It is very easily forgotten when we find ourselves locked in struggle. Neither side wants to look like a fool, not knowing, weak.

However, if one side can acknowledge "I don't know" what the best outcome is, the candor and vulnerability that enters the equation prove irresistible to the other side.

This shift is not situational; it is neurological in that we are wired to respond to what is truthful.

We cannot resist another's chosen vulnerability. We are taken over by the deeper truth that, "Neither of us knows, really."

Mountains beyond Mountains

Page 249 *Mountains beyond Mountains* by Tracy Kidder, Random House Trade Paperback 2004, about Paul Farmer and the organization he co-founded with Jim Yong Kim (and others) called Partners in Health (PIH) in 1987. Used with permission.

In this passage, Russian enemies are gathered at a fundraising dinner for PIH which is seeking funding and permission to provide health care in Russia at a time when the urban spread of tuberculosis was threatening to become a global epidemic and Russia was closed to collaboration.

The vice minister and ten big-handed Russian generals and colonels in heavy olive drab uniforms sat on one side of the assembled tables. On the other side sat the foreigners and the Russian doctors now working for PIH. The division seemed unbreachable. However, Jim had spied a TV equipped for karaoke, and as the fish course was being served I heard him whisper, "I'm gonna do it." He stood, raising his shot glass. 'I'm a terrible singer, but in my culture, Korean culture, if you respect someone and you have a deep affection and admiration for the people you're with, you should embarrass yourself by singing for them. So I will sing for you.'

"Jim belted out 'My Way.' The TV orchestra accompanied him, the words scrolled across the TV screen, and then the TV got stuck, and Jim went on alone, hitting a few sour notes. Everyone clapped, and then a member of MERLIN ... got up and sang, 'Summertime,' then a two-star general ordered up a Russian song from the TV, a lively tune, the generals and the vice minister…clapping out the rhythm…And then something rather magical happened. Without warning, and without mechanical aids., Vice Minister Kalinin himself began to sing, in a deep baritone so clear it sounded trained…and all the generals and colonels joined in…

This event resulted in bureaucratic funding and medical collaboration being granted PIH. Jim Yong Kim was credited as instrumental in turning the bureaucratic tide during that dinner.

When we know the personal and professional stakes that hold an opponent's point of view in place and we see him/her set them aside and risk ridicule, an irresistible camaraderie arises that resets the argument.

We feel held and buoyed by something beyond the argument.

We are deeply moved by stories of soldiers meeting their 'enemy' and outside the din of politics and warfare.

The children of enemies become teachers for humanity when they find each other in play.

Shakespeare's *Romeo and Juliet* never loses its power as an example of enemies' children falling in love.

Becoming a fool and singing the embarrassment, being just human and speaking the truth of one's heart, being honest when it could cost wages and more, watching another being offer us what is precious, brings us closer to our place inside the unknown, the larger.

The same occurs internally when trying to reconcile competing desires, issues or outcomes. The unknown resets the argument.

And equally so in the creative process: discarding the safe/known word, paint color or instrument more often than not frees the artistic endeavor to directly engage its audience. It seems our hearts are designed to respond to vulnerability.

Points of View (with appreciation to Suzi Tucker)

Three Papers:

one paper represents your point of view

one paper represents a point of view that is different

the third represents the unknown

Place the first two papers on the floor in a way that describes where you presently stand in relation to the different point of view.

Step onto the paper representing your point of view. Take time to notice breathing, gaze, any sensations, any desire to move from where you stand. Follow it. Experiment until you find the place that you sense is just right. Move the paper there.

Again notice breathing, gaze, sensation, emotion and/or where your focus is drawn.

After some time, move to the other paper, the point of view that is different. Here too, take time; notice breathing, gaze, any sensations, any desire to move from where you stand. Follow it. Experiment until you find the place that you sense is just right. Move the paper there.

Stay in this place, notice breath, gaze, sensation, emotion and/or where your focus is drawn.

After some time, leave this paper and go to the third paper, the unknown, yet to be placed on the floor.

See the entire floor, let your gaze move freely and without focus. Notice where you are drawn and place the paper representing the unknown there. Stand there. Take time to notice breathing, gaze, any sensations, any desire to move from where you stand. Follow it. Experiment until you find the place that you sense is just right. Move the paper there.

Return to the paper representing your point of view.

Anything change from when you first stood here? Scan breath, gaze, sensation, emotion and where your focus is drawn. Follow any interest in standing in the same place or moving.

Return to the different point of view.

Anything change? Scan breath, gaze, sensation, emotion and where your focus is drawn. Follow any interest in standing in the same place or moving.

Continue to follow movement, change a paper's placement and/or notice what occurs in each setting until the exercise feels complete.

Serendipity / Coincidence

Serendipity or coincidence is a specific group of experiences that arise for each of us regardless of morality, life position, fate, or belief.

Serendipity comes to us because we are alive. It proves the larger life and its astonishing coordinating capacity.

We are not alone and in fact we are alive inside a larger experience of life growing itself - and each of us.

The experience of coincidence is so direct, neutral and specific to the conscious and unconscious circumstances of our lives that it seems to be an answer ahead of its question or prayer. Too, each experience is so personal, immediate, and practical that we are left stunned and humbled for its direct contact.

Its experiences are not religious ones - serendipity lasts but a moment and then retreats. We are left feeling gifted, changed, connected, without need for more contact and scratching our heads.

Serendipity can reach us through plants, weather, insects, birds, animals, people, objects, movement, injury, difficulty, a sequence of unrelated events, and myriad other variables that when combined confound our imaginations.

Who or what could have fashioned such a complete response to such hidden needs? Its source seems to stand beyond definition.

Coincidence plants us directly inside the organizing source of growth. We are taken in and our outward focus is changed.

It may be our singular and most direct experience of encountering the force that sustains life.

Serendipity engages both the material and the nonmaterial worlds and creates an experience out of seemingly unrelated, a-causal components.

Its most compelling aspect is that its reach is specific to our practical lives, our minds and our emotions, with a direct action that leaves us changed, opened to more.

Coincidence gives us an experiential, momentary glimpse of the absolute unity of life and its continuous flow that includes and makes room for each of us in our specific circumstances. And its direct reach into our circumstances reminds us we are needed, just as we are.

Because we find these experiences riveting and memorable we are repeatedly persuaded to count them as part of life, albeit its mystery.

It is possible that what reaches us in serendipitous experiences as glimpse can widen into landscape in a quiet experience of our perception opening enough to let in what has always been "beyond the divide."

This possibility comes with its own doubling agent, that is, the more moments we consider life's unity, the more our awareness of it opens and in the gentlest of ways.

An inner stability takes hold and more of nature - ours and the larger - comes into view, urgency evaporates and is replaced by a constant awareness of being inside a flow that is deeper than time and wider than space.

The tremor of life's entirety moves us and all of life in ways that provide, include and connect even all that we are not yet capable of describing through language.

As life's unity becomes visible, and separation is allowed to fall away through bringing in what is not yet known to our perception, we become freer to live life's impulse to provide, include and connect in increasingly satisfying ways.

With this freedom arises a daily and self-renewing stability that brings its own peace, a peace that we'd once only imagined to be found in the hereafter.

Tone

A woman is parched with loneliness and remove. She walks to the bay and sits, watching the water. Restless and without relief, her attention moves to the shore. Stones lie next to boulders that break the water's edge. Her thoughts range from foolish for having thought a change of scenery would help, to tracking the distinct weight of nothing as it weaves its way through her torso.

Two stones draw and hold her gaze, registering in a place inside her shoulders. She tries to look away and is quickly pulled back. The magnets release their hold only while a young family crosses in front of her and sits at a nearby picnic table to share a meal. While interested, she tries not to watch them.

The stones reclaim her attention and plant a thought that will not dissolve.

Shy in front of the family yet alone enough in the landscape, she rises and walks to the stones. She changes their places, balancing one on the other, creating a small cairn. Sensing the family watching her, she looks down and leaves the area, walking back to the rooms that keep her. Isolation digs.

Days later, alone in her countenance of that day, she walks to the bay and sits on the same bench. She listens for the lap of the shallow waves and notices the pitch of sunlight from the wide sky. At least 10 minutes pass. When her gaze finds its way to the water's edge, she is curious if the two stones are still balanced.

Before her are at least 20 cairns each made of 8 to 10 stones standing within the arc of the bay.

She gasps, filled with wonder at their silent, steady watch.

A recognition reaches

her small action.   a beginning of beauty.   her timid makeup.   its constant hesitation.
helped.

This small thing I can do.   whisper.

A shiver spirals, as if of her cells.   a tone.   inexpressibly private.   finds   inside.

And she moves. relieved to tell no one.   yet more.

Sky

Were it simply opposition, coincidence and the unknown that comprised our lives, human experience would reduce itself to the simplicity of myth.

We are more than our stories and we gain perspective from our stories.

During our lives we also develop personalities, are hounded by the past and find ourselves organizing around heart, mind and or intractable circumstance.

Our mistakes and our opportunities wait for our attention.

We begin to understand that the past is cumulative and that what is not reconciled by heart lays open and affects the present circumstances until we initiate accountability.

When our days are filled with obstacles, surrender of desire is the only option that feels useful.

When other days are smooth and integrated, we feel as if we are part of the air, buoyed by a vast network that has aligned itself with our actions and desires and somehow, we with it. Inner space is outer space. And outer, inner.

Sky is our mirror.

From sky we learn we are small, connected through breath, that day follows night, and that ideas exist beyond measurement.

Surely, it is home to the not yet known.

Surely once we are inside the unknown, the un-measurable, the subtle, we are sky. .

The air in our torso is at ease.

The past called fate, the heart's attraction to love, and the daunting questions that dare us into wisdom called soul, insist we turn to them before the mirror can clear.

Injury

Injury opens us.

Beyond the impact, it awakens and then deposits the three representations of the invisible realm - fate, soul and heart – directly into our countenance and settles for nothing less than a gradual reconciliation inside and within a larger reality.

Passage to safety is gained by turning toward what hurt us (agreeing to our fate's difficulty) and asking it to teach us what we don't yet know.

This request then engages the soul's thirst for wisdom and soon shows us, as student, a wider reality and a deeper experience of growth.

As we integrate what comes into view, the heart gains in strength and resilience, becoming contributor to life with less attachment to victim.

We come to understand that injury arises as teacher, in service of what we came to learn.

The more the unchanging nature of fate is forged into acceptance;

The more soul drinks from the deeper streams of what is not yet known;

The more heart opens into its own anguish and then that of others,

The more deeply our experience of sky and its fruit of freedom, becomes.

Fate

Fate brings us into life.

We begin in circumstances difficult enough that we resist agreeing to their terms.

We begin in circumstances benevolent enough to ensure we stay alive and interested in growth.

Fate comes out of the unchanging circumstances that hold us to earth and family.

Fate waits to be folded in - accepted - into our new beings. Fate furthers life's cumulative nature.

Without respect given to the two people who brought us into our life, we will not flourish - fate is that much our starting block.

Without respect given to the bounty that gives us breath, warmth, water, food, shelter and creation, we will use (up) rather than grow into resource.

Our actions, our ancestors' actions, our eye and skin colors, the time of our birth and its location, cannot be undone. Until we agree to our beginnings - as difficult as some beginnings are - we have no sustenance from which to draw in our growth and development.

Soul

Fate collaborates with the soul's course by presenting us with the very suffering needed to open the door to our next wisdom school. It is another marvelous example of growth's movement inside every cell and impulse.

We begin life at individual and such specific starting points, in pursuit of a question whose answer can only be gained by reconciling oppositions. This question can be seen as our "wisdom school." It generates our interest, curiosity, tenacity in the face of difficulty and a constant willingness to translate injury into understanding.

In this writing, soul is the part of us that "does go with us," from one lifetime to the next. We see it in newborns' eyes - some are impossibly steady, others are filled with wonder, each distinct enough to move us to whisper, "From where did you come, little one?"

Soul not only presents us with a question, it also carries forward the wisdom gained lifetimes ago. It's how we "just know" how to assemble something, take an important action, how we "recognize" a building the first time we view it or a castle the first time we climb its stairwell.

Conversely, experiences of ineptness and whose learning is painfully slow can be seen as "first lifetime" topics that start us at the beginning, learning from every angle, as if it was an entirely new room and our presence inside it were staggeringly naive.

The question is usually clothed in opposition, riddle and paradox and is so specific that we only gradually see the relationship between fate's difficulties and the soul's riddle. When the unknown is added to the two streams of fate and soul, we begin to become teachable.

What Stays

When we first met, it was for her youngest son, a toddler. He somehow knew to climb up on the treatment table, lay on his back, and place my hand where he wanted support. I had only to follow him. She commented years later that this boy, "got his Mom in the door."

Several months later she came in for herself. Her eyes looked like a caged and tortured wild animal. She let me see them for just a moment and then resumed their downward gaze. She bolted upright on the table when I put some music on and through gritted teeth told me in so many words that music would not help.

When I took my place near the table with my senses awake to the remarkable and loud combination of life, pain and determination before me, it became clear that my hand would begin from about a yard's distance off her body.

She had equipped herself with an energetic barrier. The air changed into an intense charge closer in and became a connective transparency beyond three feet. I told her what I was feeling and that we would begin off her body. She nodded a nearly-imperceptible acknowledgement.

Most of that session was silence, a pre-verbal experience of sensing without knowing who and what was here, what was asking for attention, and what had become her tipping point as a Mom, as a wife, as a woman, daughter, human being.

Her field and her tissues were dense and reactive enough to repel any focus on details. That day began what would turn into more than ten years of being together, often in silence and at other times in response to a tentative opening. Sometimes I moved too quickly; her body's recoil and her inspiring willingness to start again, always at the ready. For more than half of those years, language was often an abrupt and raucous intruder.

Gradually she turned toward the barriers she'd developed as a child. She stood in the place of each parent and learned their limitations. She stood in her own feet and slowly came to hold her own. As the secrets made their way through her psyche, body and dream states, her gaze left the floor. She moved with more bounce, and humor became a language we shared. Life began to ask more of her wisdom.

Even so, the infrequent and paralyzing nightmares remained. During one session, she arrived desperate to unlock them; the only resource I had left was one I'd recently learned through the generational work. I offered it with trepidation that it might be misunderstood.

"There is something else that may help you. A secret energetic contract exists between perpetrator and victim. As the perpetrator takes, the victim while taken, also takes - and claims as her (or his) own, a posture of moral superiority that keeps the victim frozen, isolated and clinging to a form of emptiness."

It was as if all of her being participated in the nod that followed. A relief began its wash through her torso. Her gaze enveloped mine with a steadiness I had not yet seen. "I've always felt that but didn't know what to do with it," she stated.

As she allowed the relief to enter her nerves, blood and what separated the air between herself and others, her eyelids no longer raced, their outer edges easing.

After some time she stood. Dignity, from having told a full truth, opened its passage between her eyes and her heart.

Weeks later, she called to say the nightmares were no longer.

Fate and Soul

Fate (what I bring with me from my mother and from my father) and soul (the questions I bring from the past that includes other lifetimes), collaborate by highlighting who is missing and what remains unknown.

Our search for meaning has its origin in the confluence of fate and soul. Our inner stirrings, anxiety, and unease set our courses of growth throughout our lives.

As aspects of our personalities and our life conditions become able to flow in the river that joins fate and soul, we gain access to the deeper well of irrefutable belonging and its persistent, often hidden, expression, earth.

Fate and Soul exercise

3 papers

one represents Fate (my relationship to my past)
one represents Soul (my interest in wisdom)
the third represents the unknown

Place the first two papers on the floor in a way that describes how your past presently stands in relation to your interest in wisdom.

Do the papers face one another, are they turned away or around a corner from one another, behind or ahead?

Step on the paper representing fate. Take some time here; notice breathing, gaze, any sensations, any desire to move from where you stand. Follow it. Experiment until you find the place that you sense is just right.

Stay there and again notice breathing, gaze, sensation, emotion and/or where you focus is drawn.

After some time, move to the other paper, the one representing soul. Here too, take some time; notice breathing, gaze, any sensations, any desire to move from where you stand. Follow it. Experiment until you find the place that you sense is just right.

After some time, leave this paper and go to the third paper, the unknown, yet to be placed on the floor.

Notice the entire floor, let your gaze move freely and without focus. Notice where you are drawn and place the paper representing the unknown there. Stand there. Stay until you notice something change; it may be a thought, your gaze, a sensation, an emotion or spontaneous breath or simple boredom.

Feel free to stand in each of the places now, noting changes and similarities to the first time you stood there.

Complete by staying in neutrality, that is, without thought or action and with only a knowing you've added something new.

To this day

To this day, it is not known what brought love into being.

Perhaps it arose from the uncounted.

Perhaps from the interactions between earth, the beings and elements,

perhaps from conflict or the future.

We know only that love's effect is to bring us more,

that it enters separateness and changes our gaze forever.

And it is only humanity that has yet to solve its riddle, its koan.

Love generates what is beyond itself and leaves in its wake

a mirror stubbornly anchored beneath and next to the heart.

This mirror, whose only requirements are honesty and kindness,

waits for our gaze, collecting our instincts, tendering our needs,

providing no refuge.

We'd rather exact honesty and kindness from the other.

Impossible: each has her own path, his own path,

toward these two deepest of mirrors.

We cannot escape what beckons –

self is the most difficult to see

and the only passage we are given to other.

No matter how brief, each gaze shows us

we are broken by and beholden to life's movement.

Needs born from a heart's closure over

lifetimes, generations and yesterday, wait.

Only self-acceptance will cancel blame,

shame and pity, restoring love's flow.

Appetites, instinct and loss stand still here.

Those we've hurt pace until we call their names.

Failure upon failure - time's unchanging torment - grow heavy here.

This mirror, enough to fill a religion's hell,

waits for our heart's humbled gaze,

before and beyond any faith, law or moral

We are called to kindness and honesty,

a repeating frequency that guides our heart's migration

to relationship, diversity and the leveling effect of exposure.

As we embrace what waits broken, silence opens understanding,

As we face our failing, strength takes root and tenderness is born.

As we reject self or other, the mirror like heart, grows dim.

As we accept all that brought us here, honesty takes us into its care.

Each mirroring: how and that we dare touch one another

A cloak of life collects itself at the very edges of this reflection.

Layer inside layer we recognize self, then other then, in one another

and let fall defense, offense and reward,

choosing instead a portal, our purest experience of alchemy,

the endless passage to heart.

Heart

It is heart that sets the future in motion. It may be heart that sets the sky in motion and sky that watches after heart.

Heart is always opening toward the new, perhaps as our agent in charge of integrating what is beyond us.

Not only does heart move us toward what is new, it also collects every experience of closeness, of love.

Heart - each heart - remembers everything and everyone to whom it has opened. Given rest, it begins anew. Its depth known no limits.

All forms of separation and ending - divorce, imprisonment, loss, rejection, forgetting and breaking, show us that they are but illusions. We are always working the same issues whether in one another's company or living separately. Closeness is neither forgotten nor lost and remains a bond, tenderly showing itself in myriad ways.

When we ask our minds to forget a person, the most our hearts can do is pause.

If our minds build walls against those we've left, the former love will occupy even more space but beneath the surface of the psyche, creating its own form of bondage, as distinct from bonding; and still, the heart will not forget. It seems, heart has as its purpose, to become open, to join.

This memory and its longing can in fact continue in our blood for generations. Once the missing/exiled person is acknowledged, both hearts will seem to 'transmit' truth's relief to the family members who have followed.

We miss those from whom we separate and the missing continues until we make room for them and for the specific ways we'd opened inside the closeness. The air is impossible to divide.

Even heart's capacity to make room for those we've loved and for those who have loved us is not enough to quell soul's interest in meaning though. Soul's far and timeless reach continues in many forms. We can't shake it. Soul's stubborn capacity to wait for our attention is astonishing.

It is only soul that can bring meaning to our heart's history. When we turn toward soul and ask to learn more from the losses, more from the closenesses, to understand the value of difficulty, we will begin a journey that can teach us and cultivate meaning within a moment, often when we least expect it.

Soul's innate capacity to give meaning to our heart's suffering transforms longing/separation into wisdom. It is alchemy beyond its own definition and brings the open sky inside our torso.

It opens in us a stream that both deepens our capacity to live in difficulty purposefully and widens our commitment to staying alive. It brings with it its own particular experience of inner stability and safety too.

We settle neurologically, emotionally, physically, and within our families, communities and upon earth. We settle in a way that actually begins to utilize all that opened during our past experiences of closeness. This shows us wisdom's imperative.

Closeness is a gift that comes through others and that we ultimately deliver to ourself; if we ignore the gift then we drift farther away from the mirror of self-knowing. Our heart's ability to return to the whole and to draw from it is also diminished. We become further isolated for having turned away from an opportunity for growth. We know when we have left the whole.

We are most connected to the web of life when we welcome all who have preceded our lover, our partner, our parents, our children into our heart. They come to us out of that specific fabric. The calm that arises in this inclusive gesture suggests it is in keeping with life's design.

We are born into a web of life and held by its fibers. The fibers do not break when our hearts slam into themselves, when our partners reveal aspects we could not see. The fibers remain in place, as firmly as does our fate, our past, holding us and waiting for us to accept these people in their entirety. As acceptance dawns so too does a readiness to learn, meet, love and be loved.

We are more and more able to be life and be its expression in earth, participating in an unending blossoming.

Heart is our motherboard for growth.

Our blood holds our fate's specific frequency and it is always registering our choices and actions within sky's vast, collected rhythm.

Serendipitous experiences show us that this rhythm keeps track of each of us.

Our emotions and our perception tell us when something new is waiting to be gathered in, when we are in the "flow" and when we have deviated from it.

What drives this staggeringly complex and continuous movement? It is heart that can, like earth and sky, include all.

Seen through science, heart is a muscle, a pump whose range is incapable of reaching the tiniest of capillaries.

Seen through subtle medicine, the pump for the heart lies beyond the body, a result of the intermingling of the elements earth, air, water and fire.

Seen through the psyche, when our heart is troubled all life stands still, waiting for its restoration. And when we are falling in love, all of life can notice that the air around us has brightened.

Seen through pregnancy, our mother's blood is ours until we reach a specific point in our fetal development.

Seen through the mystic, the hands are the heart's sense organ, its reach into self and into the world.

And seen through regular eyes, we don't know what activates the pump/the heart into so many distances, directions and capacities and for so many years, across time and space.

The heart of earth may be its rock, born out of a collection of time's passage and always slowly changing, emerging.

It is difficult to write about the heart of earth (they have the same letters in english) without being faced by an enormous mystery.

Heart gathers, warms, stills, remembers, attracts, moves, registers, opens and closes, is a sense organ, an emotive center and often competes with the mind for decisions. And somehow it won't let us forget its interests.

The genesis of each of these capacities is not location specific, neither is any of these capacities measurable. We can note what they have in common and what is specific to each, aware that the not-yet-known is always in the background of heart's remarkable and far reach.

Heart remains unknowable yet is extremely sensitive to injury and new life. It takes us into new connections and thereby anchors the future. If it has an agenda or theme, it is one of moving us toward openness and ultimately each other.

A Man

I met him years later. His body was gnarled and seized in the most painful of ways. His psyche was barely his own, torn between loyalties that were as invisible as the wind yet would take him over in the fiercest of ways. Medicines held him together and they were beginning to fail.

His face usually looked tortured though when his imagination was in play, a tender-shy grin would cross his face. I would catch it from his profile and knew then that there was more to this middle-aged man than his suffering. And somehow it had survived a lifetime of struggle.

I'm not sure how I knew it was not his struggle. And yet of course it belonged to him. Maybe it was the timid smile for those brief moments, maybe it was that a certain courage surrounded the carriage of his shoulders - something that communicated an agreement to carry a burden that had become inescapable.

We are all given one. Or more - each complicated and persistent. When we think we might have escaped without burden, it arises and claims us. The past is that persistent.

This is a story about inside the heart.

When it breaks under the weight of disappointment or defeat, the pieces turn away, sigh and stop talking. The heart holds lovers, yearners, nightmares, discovery, neglect. The heart remembers everything, every moment of contact and every thwack from a bully. The heart understands time and permits denial's balm until it no longer can and then lassoes a circumstance that will state or shake the original condition forth.

There is more to the heart than its parts and this man's reaching proved it. His mind was divided and when he tried to bring it close, it simply blurred his efforts. He came from a father who was equally divided. They separately lived in their own isolated and strange wilderness.

Using a generational approach that allows parts to face one another without knowing what will follow, we sat together in silence.

When I asked the man to imagine his father, a dullness held his eyes. We waited together. After some moments, I asked him to bring his father's father into the image; his jaw began to flex though no words came forth. He then told me that he saw his grandfather wander while his father stood removed, seeming to have no sense of being a father's son.

As the moments passed, he relayed that a woman spontaneously entered his inner image and walked to within several feet of his grandfather who then turned away from her, gasping. He noticed his father's gaze had suddenly turned toward his grandfather, now a son with a stake in what would occur. The air around us split the length of the room as if broken by a pulse of fire.

The woman in the image waited. Gradually, grandfather turned to face her. I asked the man to let his grandfather say to the woman, "I can't have you." Rage, as an unbridled need to pummel the air between them, surfaced. "And for that I took you."

A flicker of relief moved through the hands of the man beside me. He bent his head forward, taking a deep private sigh.

His eyes moved as if collecting something that had fallen out of them.

His chest heaved and he stood. "I'll go now."

A silence, surely the same as must live among tall trees, the canyons and the hollows of a heart, rose with him.

Kindness and Honesty as Contribution

If there are two actions that open and link us to earth and sky, they are kindness and honesty. We arrive with them already in place. As children our gestures and observations become stories that inspire adults.

We know immediately when we are in their flow and when we have left it. We feel it in our body, mind, heart and pursuit of wisdom.

As we account and repair, we are welcomed back into a current that feels buoyant and into a stream of that at once feels personal. A specific kind of transparent assurance returns.

Kindness requires daring. It is the second half of the instruction, "Do onto others as you would have them do onto you." Once we have learned to bring kindness to ourselves, we become able offer it to others. It asks an immense leap into the unknown.

Honesty holds us to the conditions of present reality. As we practice acceptance and exposure, we gain a sense of place among humanity and upon earth. When we step away from honesty, pressures spontaneously arise to irritate us until we find our way back to our particular practice of forthrightness and accountability.

Obstacle

Three pieces of paper.

Place one on the floor to represent self.
Place another on the floor to represent an obstacle.
Place the third on the floor to represent what is unknown.

Arrange them to show their relationship to one another, i.e., is obstacle close to you, is unknown behind you?

Take some time to move the papers around until they show an image that reflects what's inside.

When you feel interested, step onto the paper for self. Notice your body, its focus, your mind, its interest, your gaze and where it's drawn, your feelings, any? and if so, familiar or different?

Once that experience has registered, step onto the paper for obstacle. Again, notice body, mind, gaze, feelings. Take your time here too.

Once that experience has registered, move to the paper that represents what is unknown.

Let the experience here reach you of its own accord.

No need to notice body, mind, gaze, feelings unless they arise unbidden.

Follow any movement that occurs to you or that interests you.

Allow in any language what arises unbidden.

Feel free to return to the other two papers, following movement, sensation and thought until the exercise feels complete.

Giving

When we visit other cultures, when we learn about other species, we notice their ways of giving, of sharing. Coyotes yip and howl to let the others know they have food to share. The most hungry of humanity daily lives the crux of having so little and a constant willingness to give to others.

The examples and experiences of being hosted by people who have little more than the meal they are sharing, change us. We have an internal monitor that tells us when it is time to give more. Giving results in less isolation for everyone, especially the giver.

There is something unexpected that occurs when we give what we'd rather keep. The material gift is replaced by a quality of non-separation. A sense of freedom enters and gentles us toward reflection about what greater force animates the bounty given, taken, received and exchanged.

What is our contribution to life?

Earth is our ground and sky is our mirror.

The measured and immeasurable are in constant interaction, one transferring its essence to the other, much the way giving what we'd rather keep does for the giver and much the way serendipity or coincidence does for the receiver.

Earth is our reference point for the material and sky is our proof of the un-measurable realms. The more we follow each example, the closer we experience the give and take of life's essence.

It is unlikely we will ever know clearly what ignites and furthers life if we continue to see humanity as owners of earth's resources or if we hold beliefs more important than direct experience.

Neither science nor religion nor politics nor culture alone is enough to demonstrate the origin of life as earth provides it and as sky furthers it. Perhaps the living of life by each of us is.

Our part, our contribution and our practice respond to a deeper order of life that is cumulative, creative and kind. The very most we can do is to live according to earth and sky's example.

When we respect ourselves and others our lives advance in a good way.

When we include the unknown, we quickly and directly experience the responsiveness of wisdom.

The practice of kindness and honesty braids fate, soul and heart.

When we look for what gathers the past, grows and makes room for the new, we see it is earth and it is sky for we notice it is their natures that flow through our human natures.

Our contribution to life occurs in the living of it as we follow earth and sky.

It is a self-paced journey that proves itself.

Made in the USA
Middletown, DE
04 December 2015